Wooden Sticks
&
Iron Men

Also by Bill Noonan

Smoke Showin'

Jakes Under Fire

Wooden Sticks
&
Iron Men

Bill Noonan

Bill Noonan

dmc associates, inc.
Dover, NH

Published by
dmc associates, inc.
P.O. Box 1095/ Dover, NH 03821-1095

ISBN:1-879848-19-8

Printed in the United States of America

1 3 5 7 6 4 2

Dedication

This book is dedicated to all the "Iron Men" of the Boston Fire Department. Most of them are gone now but I had a chance to work with some great ones. They will know who they are. It was a pleasure to go to work each tour.

And to the present and future firefighters of this great city.

Thanks!

Acknowledgments

It is never easy to put a book like this together and I would like to thank the following who have helped with this project:

Fire Commissioner Martin E. Pierce, Jr., retired, for the insightful introduction he wrote. He has been an enthusiastic supporter from the start.

Fire Commissioner Leo Stapleton, retired, for his support with this project and previous help with *Smoke Showin'* and *Jakes Under Fire*. His stories never end and they are all great.

Chief of Department Paul A. Christian for his help on the research of fires and personnel and the use of my computer. Thanks to his help, the computer is no longer just for my girls and my wife to play games on.

To all Boston Firefighters, past and present, who under extreme conditions have always done their best to protect this city from fire and other emergencies.

To my publisher, Dennis Campbell, for all his help and wisdom with this book.

To my wife, Patricia, and daughters, Coleen and Meghan; their help was immense. With photos laid out all over the floor, at times there was no place to step, but they always found that open spot! Mrs. Marie Noonan for her continued help through the years.

Bill Noonan
April 2000

Introduction

Bill Noonan is an experienced, dedicated firefighter. His knowledge and work as a photographer for the Boston Fire Department have earned him well deserved respect and recognition as one of the best photojournalists in the business.

The photos that comprise *Wooden Sticks & Iron Men* span three decades and capture events that are forever etched in our memories. These photographs present us with eyewitness accounts of bravery, courage and commitment. They recreate remarkable experiences from a bygone era, when equipment, apparatus and personal protective gear were not as advanced as they are today.

Wooden Sticks & Iron Men is a tribute to a generation of firefighters who set the standards for honor, sacrifice and accomplishment. In these pages the reader will find the reminders of the inherent dangers that these firefighters faced with every tour of duty. Although many changes have occurred over the years, the one constant is the firefighter who has helped make the world a safer and better place for all.

Martin Pierce, Commissioner
Boston Fire Department

Foreword

I think of *Wooden Sticks & Iron Men* as a photo album showing the firefighters and apparatus of the Boston Fire Department in action at various stages of fires. This is not a history book of the BFD, but a "thumbnail" look at about fifteen years of action. Some of the photos were taken while the fire was at its height, and others were taken after it was knocked down but all the apparatus were still in place.

Almost all of the apparatus had to be replaced after World War II; it was simply old. The manpower was short during the war, and large numbers of new firefighters were appointed during the years 1947-1949—over 500 in 1947 alone. So, along with new apparatus you now had eager firefighters. Most of the new firefighters were veterans.

Years ago all the ladders were wooden; the manpower had to be heavy to use this equipment. Most of the engine companies were two pieces—a hose wagon and a pump. Most wagons had permanent mounted deck guns and some also had the portable guns. These companies required many men to operate properly; they usually operated with five firefighters and an officer. On a downtown box you would get four two piece engine companies, two ladder companies, one rescue company, a water tower, the district chief and a deputy chief. That's a lot of men! Any chief officer today would love to have that response.

The first metal aerial—an American La France 125' aerial— was purchased in 1941. Two more were purchased in 1944, but these were 100' foot aerials that lasted well into the early 1970s. The 1941 aerial lasted only a few years after several tragic incidents. The wooden aerials were not dead; in 1950 Boston purchased three 85' wooden aerials from American La France. The tractors were replaced several times, but the aerials also lasted well into the mid-1970s.

Boston uses ladders extensively, primarily because the city's buildings are old and have been remodeled. There are times when the interior stairs do not follow floor patterns directly. You must have access for the firefighters working inside to get out in case there is a collapse or other problem. That is why at most large fires a ladder is placed at every floor, and at times even more are used. It was not unusual for stairs to collapse, leaving no escape from the building; ground ladders or the aerial would be only exit for firefighters.

There were a lot of rooming houses in the city and no smoke detectors. Kerosene heaters were a common source of heat, and they were frequently knocked over. If they were left on for extended periods of time, they might even explode, transforming the rooms into a deadly inferno in a matter of minutes. If there were a delay in notifying the fire department, the situation would be much more severe. It was not uncommon for some of the ladder companies to make rescues at several different fires in one week.

Several sections of the city had rooming houses that were becoming old in the 1940s and 50s. The firefighters called such housing stock "flop houses" because after an individual spent the day or the night or both drinking, he or she could get a cheap room and "flop" there. The old West End and South End had many of these types of buildings. Roxbury also had many, but they tended to be smaller structures. The ladder companies in these district both made many rescues each year. Some of these companies are not longer in service: Ladder Co. 3 and Ladder Co. 13 in the South End; Ladder Co. 12 in Roxbury; and also Rescue Co. 3 in the West End. Engine companies have also been removed from service: Engine Co. 6 in the West End; Engine Co. 26 in the South End; and Engine Co. 12, Engine Co. 13, and Engine Co. 23 in Roxbury.

A water tower usually responded to all downtown boxes on the first alarm, and usually a second tower would respond on the second alarm. The towers usually got a good spot near the front of the building. It was not at all unusual for two towers to operate at the same incident; however, I know of at least one occasion where *all three towers* operated at one fire. The only time I am aware that all four towers operated simultaneously was at a drill in April of 1948 on Dorchester Avenue, behind what is now the Federal Reserve. What a sight this must have been! Fortunately, we do have photographs of this event. The towers lost their automatic responses in 1956 but remained in reserve until the late 1960s. They could be special-called and were used at several big fires up until 1969.

As you look through and examine the photos of *Wooden Stick & Iron Men*, you will notice that at many of these fires the jakes didn't wear fire coats. Even up until the early 1970s it was not uncommon to see members of ladder companies wearing dungaree or other light jackets. After World War II many members wore the old Navy style P-coats. Boots were an option since most members had to purchase their own at that time. The only piece of personal protective gear they all wore at every fire was their helmet.

Boston Fire Department photographers took most of these photos with 4x5 Crown Graphic or Speed Graphic cameras. Some of the later photos were taken with 2¼ square film cameras. They were all firefighters assigned to the Fire Prevention Division and they processed their own film and made the photos as needed. They worked very closely with the Arson Squad. Now the phonographers are assigned to the Arson Squad.

When I was appointed to Engine Company 3 in 1971, I was fortunate to work with some of the last of the "iron men." These jakes had worked with the real "iron men"—the ones who drove the steamers and the horse-drawn ladder trucks like Ladder Co. 3 had for many years. These men knew the job inside and out, and I learned an awful lot from them, and I thank them.

I hope you'll enjoy this look back at the Boston Fire Department in action during the last days of "Wooden Sticks and Iron Men".

Bill Noonan
14 March 2000

Wooden Sticks
&
Iron Men

Water Tower 2 being fed by an old steamer, "The Abe Lincoln," (to the left, near the fence) during a fire prevention demonstration in Roxbury's Marcella Street playground. Note the hard rubber tires.
October, 1946

Water Tower 2 knocking down the fire on the fourth floor of the Chandler School for Women
at 448 Beacon Street. The building is still there; the women, however, have graduated.
Box 3-1585—June 3, 1947

This Warren Street building was the scene of several fires over the years.
One man died on the top floor in this fire.
Box 4-2131—December 22, 1947

Looking down onto Warren Street. Tower 4, Ladder Co. 3 and Ladder Co. 4.
Box 4-2131—December 22, 1947

Firefighters take a line over Ladder Co. 23's stick. Note the straight ladder on the roof.
The Roxbury Courthouse is now at this location.
Box 4-2131—December 22, 1947

The Armour Leather Company's manufacturing center on Sleeper Street was roaring when first units arrived around noon. The all day affair became an all-nighter.
Box 5-7115—January 15, 1948

Nasty! This all started as automatic alarm 416-8.
Box 5-7115—January 15, 1948

What the scene looked like coming across the Congress Street Bridge into South Boston.
Note the buff with the boots. Or is he a jake on his way to work!
Box 5-7115—January 15, 1948

Engine Co. 26's high pressure Mack wagon has both 2000 gpm guns going,
and the ice is forming on the rigs—the start of a long night.
Box 5-7115—January 15, 1948

At 4:30 PM the recall for all off-duty members was sounded...
and all on-duty members were held on.
Box 5-7115 — January 15, 1948

The next day. An aerial snapped from the weight of the heavy ice, and they brought
in the old steamer to help thaw things out.
Box 5-7115—January 12, 1948

A very cold morning on Hubert Street in Roxbury. This fire claimed one life.
Box 4-2231—January 31, 1948

Ladder Co. 4 was a 1930 America La France 85' ladder with a 1945
American La France tractor; Ladder Co. 26 was a 1944 American
La France 100' metal aerial. Here they are nose to nose.
Box 4-2231—January 31, 1948

A nice variety of rigs in a fairly typical Dorchester Street. This old service ladders were called "hayracks" by the old timers of the day.
Box 3-3336—February 12, 1948

Commissioner Codman steps over some of the spaghetti used for this
two alarm fire on Washington Street.
Box 2-1482—February 19, 1948

The view of Washington Street looking towards downtown from under the Forest Hills EL.
Box 2-1482—February 19, 1948

Chief of Department John McDonough, Commissioner Codman and his aide,
Paul Costello, confer during overhaul operations.
Box 2-1482—February 19, 1948

The market district had it all—cream, herring, eggs, paper to wrap them, and every
once in a while fire engines both old and new.
Box 3-1252—February 20, 1948

Boxe 3-1252—February 20, 1948

A 1947 Mack tractor on an 1890 KCFD 55' water tower, Tower 2
managed to squeeze into a back alley.
Box 3-1252—February 20, 1948

Time exposure captures the movements of the people and enhances the fire's intensity.
Box 3-1252—February 20, 1948

Mack high pressure wagon Engine Co. 25 operates a gun. Note the
protective cover for the wagon's hood.
Box 3-1252—February 20, 1948

Weight + ice = everybody on the forty footer.
Box 3-1252—February 20, 1948

All four water towers operating during a high pressure text on Dorchester Avenue, between Congress and Summer Streets.
April, 1948

The towers are gone, the cobblestone are gone, and so are the chiefs' Packards.
April 1948

An engine company taking a line over Ladder Co. 18's stick looks like the "up and
overs" at the Academy. Can you still get a Dawson's in Boston?
Box 3-1324—March 23, 1948

Fire in a five story granite building on the corner of South and Essex Streets,
just outside South Station, in Boston's Leather District. Three lines are
running off a high pressure hydrant.
Box 3-1434—August 27, 1948

This engine has a skid pump that was mounted on it during the war to enhance
the department's performance in case of an enemy attack.
The cop is apparently not a fire buff.
Box 3-1434—August 27, 1948

Big lines over wooden sticks on a brutally hot day. No bunker gear here!
Box 3-1434—August 27, 1948

That civilian in the upper left window seems to think the Tower has things under control.
Box 3-1434—August 27, 1948

Crew members of Rescue Co. 2 take a blow after a nasty two bagger on East Cottage Street
in Dorchester.In front, from left to right, are Jim Gallagher, John Hopkins and
Tom Curran; in the back, from left to right, are Bill Buckley,
Charlie Dewan, and, standing, Lt. Charlie Freiberg.
Box 2-3127—August 28, 1948

Chief of Department John McDonough and Deputy Chief Dan Martell at a
downtown second alarm. Only the chief of department and the
deputy chiefs wore white coats back then.
1949

Fire Commissioner Russell Codman (at top) and Chief of Department John McDonough (at bottom) direct the removal of one of two victims by the crews of Rescue Co. 3 and Engine Co. 50 from a Charlestown lodging house.
Box 2-4172—January 30, 1949

Fire Commissioner Russell Codman, Jr. responded to everything. He was the commissioner
who purchased all the Macks for the department after World War II.
Box 2-3386—July 14, 1949

A water tower washes down the upper floors of 162-168 Commercial Street, the Sunlight Banana Company's storage facility. Numerous produce wholesalers and suppliers were located in this area of the city, and many of them had serious, difficult fire over the years.
Box 2-1251—September 23, 1949

New apparatus on display at the Bowdoin Square firehouse, a truly great example of
municipal architecture that was opened in 1930 and closed in 1963.
This photo was taken around 1950.

Ladder Co. 3's chauffeur races to move the rig away as the fire blows at 117 Atkinson Street.
Box 4-3112—November 17, 1951

Water Tower 2 working on a granite block of the waterfront's Lewis Wharf...
Box 3-1245—January 28, 1952

...where eventually everything turned to ice.
Box 3-1245 — January 28, 1952

Ladder Co. 23's 1945 Mack tractor with a 1931 American La France 85'
spring-raised aerial. Five people died and eight people were injured
at this early morning Roxbury fire.
Box 3-2141—June 14, 1952

Four alarm fire at India Wharf on Atlantic Avenue. The fire began in the offices of the Gorham Fire Equipment Company. Note the cover on Water Tower 2.
Box 4-1294—June 10, 1952

Ladder Co. 4's nice 1949 Mack tractor and 1930 American La France 85' aerial and Engine Co. 26's1947 Mack wagon operate in the front of 512-520 Dudley Street, the Hodgkins Paper Company.
Box 3-3141—November 1, 1952

The Christ Church of Personal Experience on Kenilworth Street in Roxbury is really cooking.
Box 4-2252—March 19, 1953

Conditions at the church continue to deteriorate.
Box 4-2252—March 19, 1953

A jake gets into position to prepare to open up from Ladder Co. 4's spare rig...
Box 4-2252—March 19, 1953

...but worsening conditions require that he be cranked out.
Box 4-2252—March 19, 1953

Four alarm fire in a five story building on Isabella Street facing Columbus Avenue
in the South End. Numerous rescues were made over ladders
at this fire; however, five people died.
Box 4-1532—June 24, 1953

The building behind the ladders was home to American Mutual Insurance, and is still standing. The company's employees had box office seats on this day.
Box 4-1532—June 24, 1953

The *Black Falcon*, a Norwegian freighter, was docked at the South Boston Army Base
when an explosion occured in one of the holds. Seven longshoremen
were killed and thirteen were seriously injured.
Box 3-7124—November 2, 1953

The heat was so intense that the paint peeled off the side of the ship.
Box 3-7124—November 2, 1953

Engine Co. 43's wagon couldn't be much closer.
Box 3-7124—November 2, 1953

This shot has a little bit of everything—roof work, ladder work, lines in the street.
Box 3-1525—December 31, 1953

Five alarm fire at Eagle Electric Supply Co. and the Tulman Furniture store at
134 Friend Street on a bitter cold night that brought out the old steamer
in the morning to helpthaw out the apparatus and equipment.
Box 5-1321—February 1, 1954

Adams Square became one of the best fire apparatus parking lots you'll ever see for this
three alarm fire on Union Street. All the buildings to the left have been razed.
Box 3-1215 — April 26, 1954

A great shot of jakes bringing lines over ladders at a fire in a five story
apartment building at 28 Grove Street on Beacon Hill.
Box 3-1365—August 19, 1954

Chief of Department John V. Stapleton tries to explain operations to then
Fire Commissioner Francis X. Cotter.
Box 3-1514—August 26, 1954

Five story brick at 471 Tremont Street in the South End. Lines over ladder, and firefighters prepare to enter the second floor from the fire escape as another crew brings a line over a ladder to the third floor of the building in the rear.
Box 4-1525—September 19, 1954

Companies push in. Box 4-1525 — September 19, 1954

Heavy streams from the outside and the tower is prepared for operations.
Box 4-1525—September 19, 1954

Ladder Co. 8, Engine Co. 25 and Rescue Co. 3 pose after an elevator drill.
Recognize anyone here?
November 5, 1954.

If the wind had been blowing off the harbor instead of from the shore, this India Wharf
warehouse fire would have extended to other buildings.
Box 5-1257—March 3, 1955

Box 5-1246—March 3, 1955

Opening up at Gerry's Furniture in the 700 block of Washington Street.
Box 4-1491—March 14, 1955

Engine Co. 3's 1949 FWD wagon operates their deck gun at the Brighton stockyards.
Box 3-5465—April 4, 1955

The fire started in the Red Coach Grill's basement storage area. The hot, humid weather
prevented the smoke from venting.
Box 3-1547—July 1, 1955

Cots were set up for firefighters who were overcome.
Box 3-1547—July 1, 1955

A great shot of the firefighter's standard gear and equipment as Engine Co. 7 prepares
to take their turn in the basement.
Box 3-1547—July 1, 1955

Member of Engine Co. 43 wears a Chemox mask used for cellar and ship fires. Four engine squads and two additional engines were special called after the third alarm.
Box 3-1547—July 1, 1955

On a brutally hot and humid day, a firefighter from Engine Co. 18 collapsed in the attic
of this house fire. He died during transport to the hospital.
Box 3343—July 6, 1955

This fire was in a meat packing plant adjacent to the entrance to the Sumner Tunnel.
The scene looks like an advertisement for Marck apparatus.
Box 2-1252—August 25, 1955

Look at what's missing! The skyline has definitely changed.
Box 2-1252—August 25, 1955

A couple of four story wood structures on a Roxbury street caused a bit of commotion.
Box 3-2235—December 6, 1955

The captain of Engine Co. 3 says, "We gotta get a line over there. The exposure's going." An early morning fire in a four story apartment building on West Broadway in South Boston.
Box 5-7137—December 12, 1955

Engine Co. 43's gun is starting to work on the rear of this fully involved
apartment house. Three people died in this fire.
Box 5-7137—December 12, 1955

Heavy smoke from the front of the house on West Broadway.
Box 5-7137—December 12, 1955

A fire in a coal elevator—a thing of the past!—on Quincy Street in Dorchester.
Engine company member is waiting for water on the gun.
Box 2-3175—January 6, 1956

Engine Co. 8 with a line over a ladder to the top floor of an East Boston warehouse.
Box 3-6135—January 18, 1956

Smoke turns to steam as companies get a handle on the fire.
Box 3-6135—January 18, 1956

Whose turn is it to feed the meter?
Box 3-1471—February 3, 1956

Ladder Co. 12's 1955 FWD tractor and 1950 American La France 85' wooden aerial
at a typical Roxbury tenement fire at 552 Shawmut Avenue.
Box 2-2217—February 221, 1956

Four alarm fire at 1866 Commonwealth Avenue, Brighton. Looks like a 50' ladder
to the front; it takes at least six guys to do this properly.
Box 4-5352—May 2, 1956

Ladder Co. 11's 1944 American La France 100' aerial and
Ladder Co. 14's 1949 FWD 85' aerial.
Box 4-5352—May 2, 1956

Ladder Co. 13's stick has a great spot.
Box 3-2112—August 25, 1956

Ladder Co. 12's 1955 FWD tractor with a 1950 American La France spring-raised 85'
aerial makes it into the back. You have to wonder how they got it out!
Box 3-2112—August 25, 1956

Deck guns out front at this five alarm fire in East Boston.
Box 5-6213—November 8, 1956

The scene of Saratoga and Curtis streets seen from the McLellan Highway.
Box 5-6213—November 8, 1956

Engine Squad 11 with a gun to the top floor, and Engine Co. 25's
wagon shoots between the buildings.
Box 5-6213—November 8, 1956

Out back, Engine Co. 40's wagon 1950 Mack with a deck gun.
Box 5-6213—November 8, 1956

Ladder Cos. 12 and 8 respond to a four alarm fire at 82 Atlantic Avenue.
Both companies are now out of service.
Box 4-1246—November 15, 1956

Don't think they'd use Atlantic Avenue as a train yard anymore. And the passersby seem
completely oblivious to this four bagger!
Box 4-1246—November 15, 1956

Ladders and fire escapes and Ladder Companies 13 and 12
side by side; both companies are now gone.
Box 3-1554—December 26, 1956

Back to basics: lines over ladders on the corner of Columbus Avenue and Worcester Street.
Box 3-1554—December 26, 1956

We saved the First Church of Charlestown Congregational on Green Street. Note the
tiller seat swung out of the way to throw the stick.
Box 5-4141—January 12, 1957

Engine Co. 36's 1950 Mack "Cardox" wagon with gun operating.
Box 5-4141—January 12, 1957

Engine Co. 3 with a line over Ladder Co. 22's stick, a 1950
American La France 85' wooden spring-raised.
Box 5-4141—January 12, 1957

This was a three alarm fire at Federal Liquors on Chardon Street. Lots of different rigs, but the trucks always got the front of the building.
Box 3-1331 — March 25, 1957

An engine company operates a big line off Ladder Co. 1's stick.
Box 3-1331—March 25, 1957

Chardon Street is absolutely clogged. Note the high pressure hydrant on the left sidewalk;
also, the protective guy in the center running with the covers.
Protectives have been gone since 1959.
Box 3-1331—March 25, 1957

Companies push in working off the sticks.
Box 3-1331—March 25, 1957

Federal Liquors was really stocked! Engine companies have knocked down
the fire and are using 1½" lines to finish up.
Box 3-1331—March 25, 1957

First comes the smoke near the Dudley Street EL station...
Box 4-2234—April 17, 1957

...then comes the fire as jakes prepare to hit it from the EL.
Box 4-2234—April 17, 1957

You don't see this every day: two 1 ½ " lines off a portable deck gun. An Engine Co. 3 idea.
Box 4-2234—April 17, 1957

Three and a half story dwelling with a Mansard roof. Wooden ladders have given way
to metal at this Shawmut Avenue fire
Box 3-2231—April 21, 1957

Engine Co. 3 hits between these three deckers at a four alarm fire on Woodcliff Street
and Howard Avenue in Dorchester.
Box 4-1785—May 2, 1957

Engine Co. 21 hits between several others. Note the overhead ladder rack with 35' ladder.
Box 4-1785—May 2, 1957

Engine Co. 3's hose wagon. After they had their lines charged, they drove the length
of the building and knocked down most of the heavy fire...
Box 5-1563—March 29, 1958

...making this a kind of one company five alarm fire!
Box 5-1563—March 29, 1958

These burning Boston & Albany Railroad sheds stood where the Prudential Center now stands.
Box 5-1563—March 29, 1958

Members wearing Chemox masks prepare to enter *USCG Eastwind* at the Castle Island Terminal
Box 2-735 — April 17, 1958

Fire in a five story commercial building on Summer Street that was the home
of Rosoff's Restaurant, a favorite downtown eatery.
Box 3-1431—May 6, 1958

Lots of ladder work at an early morning fire that claimed three people on
Staniford Street in Boston's old West End
Box 3-1352—May 7, 1958.

Rain doesn't slow down the job; it just makes the job wetter.
Box 3-1352—May 7, 1958

This fire started on the street behind and extended to these houses.
Box 3-3446—September 12, 1958

Ladder Co. 29's 1950 Mack 65' aerial is up and ready.
Box 3-3446—September 12, 1958

A backdraft at this fire on Blackstone Street, downtown, caught several firefighters
and blew them out of the building; others had to be rescued. Several
members were seriously injured; one never returned to duty.
Box 3-1258—March 27, 1959

This was a four alarm fire on a pier off Summer Street. The fireboats were able to operate,
but the strong wind sure didn't help. Ladder Co. 18's 1957 Mack tractor/
1944 American La France aerial has been moved out of danger.
Box 4-7123—August 3, 1959

The crew of Engine Co. 12 pose before making up at the two alarm fire on Warren Street.
The lieutenant is holding the officer's Wheat light, which was standard for many years.
Members are Pete Umile, Fred Smith and John Gegan standing in the back,
and John Sheedy and Lt. Joe Anderson in front.
Box 2-2127—August 17, 1959

This fire on Washington Street, across from Jordan Marsh, is really juicy!
Looks like it's ready to blow...
Box 4-1461—February 13, 1960

Here it comes...everyone back down.
Box 4-1461—February 13, 1960

Companies back down the stick. We'll have to hit it from here.
Box 4-1461—February 13, 1960

Many rescues were made during this cold morning. Heavy snow hampered firefighters
during this blaze on Symphony Road in the Back Bay section of the city.
Box 2-2323—March 6, 1960

This fire was in an occupied four story apartment building at the corner of Forest and Vine Streets in Roxbury. Firefighters made many rescues, but two people died.
Box 3-2135—May 11, 1960

A man was found on the top floor and pulled out...
Box 3-2135—May 11, 1960

...and handed to Lt. Hardy of Ladder Co. 12.
Box 3-2135—May 11, 1960

Another victim is removed from the third floor.
Box 3-2135—May 11, 1960

Lt. Gerry Flemming of the Rescue Company and a firefigter remove a body from
the upper floor of a South End rooming house.
Box 2-1614—March 1, 1961

Some things will never change! Fire at 212 Beacon Street, Back Bay.
Box 2-1578—March 11, 1961

The fire began in a junk yard on Harrison Avenue in Roxbury—directly across from what is now
Harrison Supply—and extended to numerous buldings.
Box 4-2123—June 5, 1961

Four alarm fire at the Castle Island terminal in South Boston. All Multiple Alarms were ordered by Chief of Department John A. Martin; he waswalking Castle Island at the time.
Box 4-735—November 30, 1961

The creosote-soaked timbers burned for three days.
Box 4-735 — November 30, 1961

Did you ever think you'd see cellar pipes at a pier fire?
Box 4-735—November 30, 1961

The BFD fireboat *Joseph J. Luna*—Engine Co. 47—operates rail guns, but it doesn't
seem to be making much progress.
Box 4-735—November 30, 1961

Deputy Chief Fred Clauss, Firefighter Andy Brady, E-3, and Lt. John Campbell, L-3, attend an injured woman at a fire in a four story residence on Shawmut Avenue. Box 2-2231—January 6, 1962

Engine Co. 3 on the fire escape of a five story apartment building on Beacon Hill's
South Margin Street. One resident died in this morning fire.
Box 3-1337—March 17, 1962

The old Elm Building on Hanover Street—located approximately where Boston City Hall now stands—was being demolished when this four alarm fire broke out.
Box 4-1323—April 22, 1962

One tower working, one tower getting ready, and one ladder pipe
going at it. The old and the new!
Box 4-1323—April 22, 1962

This fire was right in Brigham Circle, at Tremont Street and Huntington Avenue.
Box 3-2355—May 23, 1962

Hey, these are some pretty good prices!
Box 3-2355—May 23, 1962

Ladder Co. 13's 1958 Seagrave 100' aerial makes it to the side.
Box 3-2355—May 23, 1962

The potato shed fires roared in the Charlestown train yards and
extended to houses across the street.
Box 5 + - 4132—May 10, 1962

A jake pulls fence down with a Halligan bar to improve access.
Box 5 + - 4132—May 10, 1962

Do you think this jake's sneaking through the fence to see if the spuds are done?
Box 5 + - 4132—May 10, 1962

This Charlestown paper company posed a different set of problems. Love that Mack tractor.
Box 4-417—July 13, 1962

Deck guns do what they can at a four bagger at the American Packers Box Company
on Medford Street in Charlestown.
Box 4-4164—September 3, 1962

Access was a problem during this five alarm fire at the vacant Frothingham School on Charlestown's Prospect Street, a stone's throw from the Bunker Hill Monument.
Box 5-4143—October 15, 1962

Another vacant five story building on Brattle Street—part of the area that was
redeveloped for the Government Center.
Box 3-1259—March 2, 1963

Five alarm fire at the Sherry Biltmore Hotel on the corner of Mass. Ave. and Belvidere Street.
Box 5-2321—March 29, 1963

Jakes made over eighty rescues over ladders at this fire;still, four people died
and twenty-seven were injured.
Box 5-2321—March 29, 1963

Ten ladder companies operated at the Sherry Biltmore fire.
Box 5-2321—March 29, 1963

The Sherry Biltmore was one of the most extensive laddering jobs in the history
of the BFD. Air conditioners in windows hindered rescue efforts.
Box 5-2321—March 29, 1963

The view looking up Belvidere Street, towards Mass. Ave. Note the numerous
ladders placed on the building's overhangs.
Box 5-2321—March 29, 1963

The scene on Mass. Ave. itself, looking towards Cambridge. This building
is now part of the Berklee School of Music.
Box 5-2321—March 29, 1963

Fire in an old granite block warehouse building on Commercial Street. The Tower is working again with Ladder Co. 8's 1956 100' Seagrave and Ladder Co. 18's 1957 Mack with a 1944 American La France 100' aerial.
Box 4-1251—September 11, 1963

The rear of the warehouse on Fulton Street.
Box 4-1251—September 11, 1963

Jakes bring a line over the stick to the fourth floor on the Fulton Street side.
Box 4-1251—September 11, 1963

Ladder Companies 1 and 24 are almost nose to nose on the Fulton Street side.
Box 4-1251—September 11, 1963

The fire started in the Morgan Memorial complex on Shawmut Avenuen and Corning Street and quickly extended to other buildings. This fire actually went to five alarms in five minutes.
Box 5 + -1611—October 12, 1963

Given the circmustances, would you or would you not turn your helmet around?
Is that your final answer?
Box 5 + -1611—October 12, 1963

The view up Shawmut Avenue towards downtown. The Hotel Bradford
can be seen in the background.
Box 5 + -1611—October 12, 1963

Box 5 + -1611—October 12, 1963

Six million gallons of acetate were flowing from railroad cars on the tracks adjacent to Western Avenue in Brighton—a serious haz-mat incident.Of course, who had a Haz-Mat Unit in 1963! The 2nd and 4th alarms were skipped.
Box 5-5276—October 25, 1963